The Liquid Bible

Recapturing the Flow of the Great Story of God

BY PAUL THOME

ISBN: 1439266018
ISBN-13: 9781439266014
Library of Congress Control Number: 2009911924

Dedication

To my family: the love of my life, Sherri,
Alisha and Brandon, Brooks and Jennie,
Mason, Carter, Ellie, and Jesse

I am a rich man because all of you are in my life.
Thank you for your love, your support through the years,
your active encouragement, and your belief
that God has a unique contribution for me to make in advancing
Jesus' kingdom in this world.

8 children

Acknowledgments

This book would not exist without the unflagging support of my wife, Sherri, the constant encouragement of my children, Alisha and Brandon, Brooks and Jennie. You were my constant cheering section, and I am forever grateful for your love, undeserving as I am.

There are so many people—too numerous to mention—who made contributions both to my development as an individual and to this work itself, and who deserve recognition of one kind or another. That being the case, I'd like to mention a few of those key people in my life, though by no means is this list exhaustive.

Obviously, my entire extended family has exerted a huge influence on my life and work—my father and mother, Paul and Carolyn Thome, who gave me life and nurtured me throughout my early years; my father and mother-in-law, Kirk and Connie Davis—thanks for your love, prayers, and encouragement. Tim and Terry Dakin, you kept my spirits up through many difficult ministry challenges and always provided a listening ear. A special thanks goes to Art Vanderveen, who will probably never realize how seminal his influence was to this work. Art taught a Bible overview course to a group of college students at Campus Crusade's International School of Biblical Studies in Cuernavaca, Mexico, in the summer of 1973. I was one of those students, and that course changed my life and ministry. Most of the concepts and ideas for *The Liquid Bible* came directly from that class. I still have the notes! Bill Steel, my youth pastor at Fair Oaks Presbyterian Church—you left your mark on me in ways I cannot even begin to count.

I'd especially like to thank Kristin Lyle for her sharp editorial eye and her hilarious wit. Additional thanks go out to my nephew Todd Dakin, as well as Ashleigh Elser, Jonathan McKee, Linda Miller, and Chad Hall, who served as early readers and gave me invaluable feedback regarding the structure of parts of the book. In fact, Chad coached me into the "next step" of getting it published. Dr. Tom Tunnicliff was one of my earliest cheerleaders—thanks for your encouragement and actually using the earliest version of the manuscript to train your leaders at Sun River Church, Sun Grove Community Church, and Arcade Church. Finally, a special shout-out goes to the congregations of Sun Hills Community Church and Sun River Church, two spiritual communities that allowed me to pastor them and teach the scriptures to them for the past twenty-eight years. I am both humbled and thrilled to have had the opportunity to serve both of you.

Author's Note

Over the years, I've had the honor of holding open conversations with spiritual seekers as well as veteran followers of the Christian faith. With few exceptions, most found themselves stuck in their journey because they could not overcome the inherent difficulties in reading and attempting to understand the Bible. I, myself, shared the same struggle in the beginning of my own spiritual journey. This, of course, was pretty disturbing for me personally, as I'm sure it is for many. I knew that the Bible claimed to be one of the most potent spiritual resources anyone can take advantage of in his or her journey of faith. All the data on spiritual growth and transformation clearly indicate that spending time with the Bible is, hands down, the most productive and impactful of all personal, spiritual practices. Yet, millions of people find themselves confused—thus disinterested and unmotivated—and as a result, reluctant to use this powerful, spiritual resource. I, myself, wanted to understand the Bible better, but at times the process seemed so tedious.

My own struggle was stopped cold by a simple discovery—a clear, concise understanding of the basic flow of the story of the Bible. I don't know how to explain this, but it somehow ignited something in my soul. I found myself highly motivated to read, understand, and then begin to apply the Bible's truths to my life. In time, my progress led me to develop and fine-tune a resource to help others discover what I'd discovered, which eventually evolved into this book, *The Liquid Bible*. *The Liquid Bible* is a resource designed to help anyone get a firm grasp of the basic flow of the Bible as a story in order to connect more deeply with the message it holds for us and to connect more deeply with the God who lives within its pages. This can be absolutely life-changing.

My hope is that *The Liquid Bible* will expose spiritual seekers to the essential message of the Bible and inspire them to discover and embrace the God who is described within its story. At the very least, I hope it will give them accurate information about who God is and about His plans and purposes for them as human beings, so they can make an informed, intelligent decision about the role they will let Him play in their lives.

Beyond this, I hope more advanced learners will use it to develop a solid, foundational framework for a lifetime of spiritual learning and encouragement. They may even find it a valuable resource for helping younger, less-developed followers build a stronger spiritual foundation as well.

GETTING THE MOST FROM THIS BOOK

✓ Read it all the way through. While this may seem obvious, how many of us start books and don't finish them?

✓ Sit down with a piece of paper ahead of time and practice drawing the "Bible on a napkin" diagram—say, about five times. This will imprint the flow of the story in your mind, and you'll have more fun recognizing the high points of the story as you read.

✓ There's one more feature I've provided that I want to point out to you. At the end of each chapter, I've included some of the primary portions of the Bible that "carry" the major plot points of the story. I've creatively called them—you guessed it—"Plot Points." These are the critical passages on which the story of the Bible turns. I highly encourage you to read each of them as you finish each chapter. It may seem ridiculously elementary, but it seems to me if we really want to "get" the essential message of the Bible, it only makes sense that we should actually read at least some of it firsthand.

So get ready to jump in and get caught up in the powerful current of the story of all stories—the great story of God.

Table of Contents

Preface

He said it right to my face without hesitation. And he meant it. "I just don't get it—at all."

"What do you mean by that?" I asked.

"The Bible. I mean, it's gotta be the most boring thing on the planet, next to watching grass grow."

I was sitting across the table from a young man in his late twenties. He sported tats up one forearm to the sleeve, two earrings in his left ear, and a sparse goatee. He had intelligent eyes, complemented by a soft smile. This young man was in the midst of a serious spiritual search, so we'd met at a local coffee shop to talk. Apparently I was someone he thought could provide some answers. We'd soon see.

We'd been talking about whether there was any empirical evidence—tangible, concrete, beyond- reasonable-doubt reasons—for the existence of a real, "capital G" God.

"How much of it [the Bible] have you read?" I asked.

"Well, that's just it. I've tried. I've really tried. But I don't get very far before I'm absolutely lost," he replied. "So then I just skip to another part, but the same thing happens. It's all about a bunch of people and places and things I can't relate to and, frankly, couldn't care less about. After a while, it all just starts to sound the same. Everything about it is strange." He shook his head slightly side to side as he finished—just for emphasis.

He checked my face, took a sip of his coffee, lowered the cup to the table, and then said, "Can I be real honest with you? Look at it. It's huge! Over a thousand flippin' pages, man! And complicated, too. It's filled with all kinds of information that's obscure and cryptic—like family trees, and ancient rituals, and God speaking to people in audible voices and miraculous signs and stuff. It feels like the people are from another planet, the writing style is archaic, and the language is clunky. Shakespeare is easier to read and understand.

"And it doesn't read like a regular story or a novel. It's not even in chronological order. I had an easier time following the movie *Memento*. When I read some of the stories, I feel like I'm a little kid being asked to believe in fairy tales. It just doesn't feel believable to me. I have friends who call themselves followers of Jesus, and even they say it's a load to read and understand, though they do admit that they are occasionally inspired by it. And I can see that. I've gotten a few good feelings out of it myself. But mostly, I sorta feel like 'why try?' There just doesn't seem to be enough bang for the buck."

He sighed and then continued. "I'm not sure it has anything meaningful to say to me, not in this day and age." He said it like someone who'd just played the lottery, discovering he'd dialed in all the numbers correctly except for the last one.

For a moment, we were both silent as we sipped our drinks. Cups clinked and espresso machines exhaled around us. I looked out the window and watched cars snake past on the street outside.

"You're right, man," I finally admitted. "Dead on. Let's face it. It is a very large book. The language is ancient, the people act weird, and the culture and times are completely dated. The writing styles are foreign, and it doesn't read easily."

He lifted an eyebrow at me with something like surprise. I guess my response had clearly not been on his radar screen.

"But there's this verse in the Bible that I can't get past, either. In the wisdom literature of Proverbs, it says, *'It is the glory of God to conceal a matter, and it is the glory of kings to search it out.'*" I let that sink in for a few moments and then continued. "There is something about this book that requires us to read it deliberately, not casually—not like a novel that we pick up, read, and easily forget. Instead, it seems more like reading a good murder mystery where important clues are sprinkled throughout the storyline. What if God intended for us to have to stretch our minds and our hearts a little before we could fully realize and clearly understand the message inside? What if God never intended for this book to be easy, but in fact to be the challenge it is—something that would separate genuine seekers from half-hearted wannabes? What if He wanted to force us to think harder about what it says so that He could bring out the best of what He's placed inside of us? What if a good part of the Bible's real value is how it forces us to wrestle with its message in such a way that it puts us in touch with the very heartbeat of the God who inspired it?"

I could feel my pulse quicken a tiny bit even as I said it.

"I keep reminding myself that the Bible is the best-selling book of all time—and not without reason," I continued. "Hidden within the pages of this book is the spiritual code for life. It carries a timeless message that can open us up to the God who is the source of life like nothing else around. This book carries uncommon wisdom that's practical and relevant for our world today. It can help people overcome addictions;

build strong, vital marriages; raise healthy families; heal traumatic wounds; restore relational breakdowns; face unimaginable challenges; and alter eternal destinies. It is the primary truth-source that leads us toward God—and toward a rediscovery of His blueprint for a life that never quits, fades, loses strength, or ends. The Bible has given people this kind of hope and strength through at least two millennia plus. It's still doing this in the lives of real people today."

I'd noticed my friend shifting in his chair a little. He sat forward slightly, his eyes holding my gaze, and I thought I noticed some kind of spark that hadn't been there before.

So I kept right on going. "I think one of the reasons most people misunderstand the Bible is that they don't know how to read it right. What I mean is they haven't read it through the times, the languages, the cultures, the literary styles of the times, and the historical settings in which it was written. These are fundamental literary principles we apply to every other kind of literature from every period in history, from *The Odyssey* to Shakespeare to *Harry Potter*. But when we get to the Bible, it seems like we ignore them then wonder why it seems so dull.

"But beyond all that stuff, I believe the average person doesn't get the Bible, or 'get into' the Bible, largely because he or she simply doesn't understand the basic flow of the story. Tragically, most people have only been exposed to the Bible in 'bytes.' They may know about a few events or facts here, or maybe they've heard a couple of 'Bible stories' there, but they have no idea how those parts flow, fitting together into a cohesive, integrated whole. As a result, the book seems stale, jumbled, incoherent, and disjointed. So they avoid it like the plague."

"Well, that's me," he deadpanned.

"But, if you could somehow get an overall sense of the flow of the story, all that could change," I said. "See, at its core, the Bible is liquid—a fluid narrative telling the essential story of our world. Like a massive river that starts somewhere and moves somewhere else, it is the story of God and of our lives, a story that flows strong and powerful and beautiful. At times, it is turbulent and vicious and messy. At other times it is clear and calm. It moves, it twists and turns, expanding and contracting, but always flowing toward a larger reality bigger than ourselves."

We were both quiet again. After a moment, he said, "Let me ask you something." The knuckles of his right hand came to rest just under his chin, elbow resting on the table—à la Auguste Rodin's "Thinker." "Do you think that if people were able to get some kind of basic orientation to the story of the Bible, that maybe it could somehow not only hold their interest, but also help them understand it and actually get something out of it?"

"I do," I replied.

We sat for a moment, both of us lost in thought for a little while, until he said, "Is there anything out there that does that? Any book that puts a little more meat on the bones without overdoing it, without getting too detailed, technical, theoretical, or theatrical? Maybe a 'Cliff Notes' version of sorts?"

I thought for a moment.

"Hmmm. Not that I'm aware of," I replied. "Most of the *Idiots* or *Dummies Guide* stuff is still pretty long—I mean, like a couple hundred pages or more—and most of them are still largely academic in their approach. Remember, the Bible is primarily a story told through the lives of real people living in a real world, wrestling with what it means to trust a real God, and told through a lot of different literary mediums: stories, genealogies, court records, letters, poetry, prose, and parables. Nothing I know of out there tries to tell it as a simple story. Somewhere along the line, I think it should be told and understood as a story—a story that is continuous, alive, moving, flowing. I think this is where its true power lies."

The wheels in my head were spinning. An idea was taking shape.

"You know, if someone could do that," I said, "tell the whole story of the Bible from beginning to end in chronological order, simply, yet intelligently—and accurately—that would be huge, wouldn't it? I mean that could be a big-time help to people in overcoming the inherent obstacles and mystery surrounding the Bible. I think more people might connect with it better, read it, maybe get into it more—and get more out of it, too!"

"Dude, if there were something like that, I'd sure be willing to check it out," he said, sitting back and running his hands through his hair.

Picking up on his previous statement, I made a proposal. "Let me show you something. Give me your napkin…"

I began to draw a small diagram on it that looked something like this:

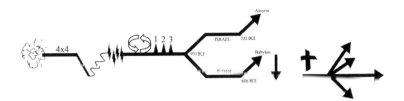

As I drew, I said, "This represents the entire storyline of the Bible."

"Okay," he said when I finished. "You gotta be kidding me. That's pretty simple."

"Yeah, I have a friend who calls this 'the Bible on a napkin.' But remember," I said, "this is only an overall orientation to the basic story-line—it's supposed to be really simple. However, with this diagram, I not only can tell you the entire story of the Bible in about seven minutes, I can also help you remember it better."

"No way!" he shot back.

"Way," I said. "At least I can give you the bare-bones version. But it would be better to have it in written form, with a little more detail because the more meat you put on it, the more meaningfully it will speak to you."

After a moment, he sat forward in his chair, his eyes boring into mine. "Could we do that? I mean could you help me do that? Help me understand the simple storyline of the Bible?"

"Sure!" I replied. "Here, take the napkin and follow along with me. It all begins right here with the beginning of the world as we know it…"

Chapter One: Back in the Day

If you've ever walked into a movie after it's already begun, you know how frustrating it can be to try to catch up and follow the story. You have no idea who the characters are, don't know what's been going on, who belongs to whom, or why they say and do some of the things they do. As a result, the plot is hard to pick up and doesn't make much sense. When the plot is fuzzy, your interest level goes way south. Like most things in life, you want to experience it from the beginning.

That's where the Bible begins.

The story of the Bible starts with the origins of our universe as we know it. This beginning is found in the opening chapters of the Bible—in the book called Genesis ("beginnings"). The first eleven chapters trace its foundational origins through four major historical events: Creation, the Fall of Man, the Flood, and the Tower of Babel.

CREATION

The Bible shamelessly declares that God Himself created our known universe. Through a series of verbal commands, God spoke into existence an ordered, fine-tuned universe of precision, symmetry, beauty, color, diversity, and life. Genesis tells us that God first **formed** the universe and then **filled** it with life. The greatest expression of life God created was human life—the first humans being Adam and Eve, who initially represented the entire human race to come after them. Human beings were God's opus—His greatest creative masterpiece. The man and woman were originally created to know God personally, love Him, grow in their relationship with Him, and become co-creators of the human race. He custom-designed them to represent Him on the earth and assigned them the responsibility of managing His world according to His goals, plans, and purposes. God gave the man and the woman everything they needed in order to carry out this task: their distinctively superior faculties, their gifts, talents, time, resources, aptitudes, and abilities. All these uniquely human attributes were designed to be energized and activated by an inner spiritual connection with God—by the very life of the Creator Himself. This inner connection would remain solid and free-flowing based on their perfect trust in Him to provide everything they would ever need. God then placed them in an idyllic environment called the Garden of Eden. Like parents who lovingly and thoughtfully prepare a nursery for a newborn infant, God crafted a universe that would provide the optimum environment for the growth and development of human life. All Adam and Eve had to do was to stay fully connected to God by trusting Him and following Him perfectly.

THE FALL

One day, however, the man and the woman made a fatal decision to trust in themselves rather than God. Tempted by a serpent (a reptile representing a very real spiritual enemy whom the Bible calls Satan), Adam and Eve chose to reject God's leadership in their lives and ate from the only tree in the garden that God had designated "off limits" to them.

The problem wasn't the fruit itself. The problem was their spirit of independence from God. This attitude of trusting themselves instead of God is the core definition of what the Bible calls "sin." Instead of relying on God's directives as the basis for knowing good and evil, they relied on their own innate ability to discern good and evil, right and wrong, and ate from the tree of the knowledge of good and evil, thus committing cosmic treason against Him. Because Adam and Eve represented the human race fully, their decision is representative of the same decision all human beings either have made or will make at one time or another in their lives: the intentional decision to live their lives on the basis of their own strength, their own wisdom, and on their own terms without God.

As a result, Adam and Eve's whole world unraveled. Their decision ruptured their inner, spiritual connection with God, fundamentally putting them at odds with Him. The integrity of their lives was fractured at its core. They found themselves disconnected from God and out of sync with themselves, with each other, and even with the environment around them. Without God's cohesive, integrating presence in their lives, they became broken, flawed, foolish, and defective—in a word, lost.

In spite of this, God reached out to them in two acts of care and compassion. First, He made them a promise. He promised them that the human race would not remain this way forever. Someday, He would again raise up a single human representative who would conquer sin, evil, and death once and for all (Genesis 3:15). Second, He graciously removed them from the Garden, so they could not eat from the tree of life (also in the Garden) and thus live forever as broken, defective, lost people. Adam and Eve entered an existence drastically different from the one God had originally intended for them.

THE FLOOD

In time, through Adam and Eve, the human race multiplied. Although some individuals sought after God and tried to follow Him as closely as possible, eventually man's defective nature metastasized, infecting human beings so comprehensively and deeply that it dominated the entire race. The infection became so severe that God decided to destroy human life and start over again. But instead of starting from scratch, God chose a righteous man, Noah, and his family to become the foundation of a new human race. God instructed Noah to build a huge boat—called an ark—which Noah spent close to the next eighty years constructing. When it was finished, God spoke to Noah, telling him and his family to gather a representative collection of all the species in the animal kingdom and to enter the ark. God then sent a massive rain that flooded the earth and destroyed all land-based life on it. After a period of forty days, the rains stopped. Roughly a year later, when the waters had finally receded, Noah and the animals left the ark and began the task of repopulating the earth again—each species according to its kind.

THE TOWER OF BABEL

After Noah, the human race again multiplied, but it was the same story all over again. The inclination to be independent from God and depend on their own natural, human resources had become so deeply ingrained in human nature that men and women began to drift further and further away from God again. Determined to build their own lives and their own world without God, they made plans to build a great tower as a monument to human strength, creativity, and ability. This tower (now known as the Tower of Babel) would be a symbol of man's superiority and independence from God. Seeing the damage such an attitude would have on the human race, God stopped the project cold by confusing the universal language spoken at that time. Since the workers could no longer communicate with each other (they were described as "babbling," hence the name "Babel"), the project went toes-up. In time, groups of people who spoke similar dialects hooked up with each other and formed homogenous communities, eventually moving away from other groups and scattering over the face of the earth.

We call this beginning period of the story the *Primeval Period*. Remember, this period revolves around four universal events: *The Creation, the Fall, the Flood,* and *the Tower of Babel*. Remember these four events—they form the first **"4"** in the napkin diagram.

That's the beginning chapter of the story. As you can see, there's an emerging pattern in these four events. In each event, God deals universally with the world as a whole. He patiently continues to work with flawed, resistant, lost human beings time and time again. He loves them, but He loves them too much to give up on them or leave them as lost, sinful, separated, and scattered. The Bible is the phenomenal story of God pursuing His great dream: to permanently recapture the hearts of lost people, bring them back home again someday, and reunite them with one another in a new spiritual family, which would someday comprise a new humanity. The word we use to describe this grand purpose is *redemption*. This is the underlying current of the entire story, and it shapes the flow of almost everything the great story of God is about.

Plot Points: **Genesis 1–3**

Genesis 6:11–8:22

Genesis 11:1–9

Chapter Two: The Four Fathers of Faith

Genesis 12 marks a new phase in God's dream to reclaim and redeem His lost world—the birth of the nation of Israel. In an effort to bring the scattered peoples of the earth back together again, God planned the creation of a *model nation*—an ethnic group of people so connected to Him, so in tune with His goals, values, ideals, and agenda, and so committed to Him that they would act as a living model of His life and character to the world. Not only would they be a model nation, they would also be a *magnet nation*, attracting all the other nations of the earth to join them in becoming a part of God's spiritual family. From this nation, God intended to one day raise up the Messiah—that single, human representative He'd promised Adam and Eve, and who would one day conquer the power of sin and evil forever.

In order to be a legitimate nation, you have to start with the element of a *common people*, that is, a group of people who share a common ethnic origin, heritage, and legacy. This would be God's starting point for the next phase of the story.

I call this section of the Bible the **Four Fathers**, represented by the second "**x 4**" in the diagram. This part of the story traces the beginnings of the nation of Israel through four successive generations, anchored around four individuals: Abraham, Isaac, Jacob, and Joseph.

Abraham: Abraham, originally named Abram, is a picture of *God's sovereign calling* because God called him out of a totally secular culture in Ur (present-day Iraq) to begin a relationship with Him and to establish that relationship in the land of Canaan (present-day Palestine). God promised Abraham that he would become the father of a new nation and that the land of Canaan would someday belong to his descendants. Abraham completely trusted God for these two promises.

Abraham had a son named **Isaac,** who is a picture of *God's sovereign conception*. Isaac was born to Abraham and his wife, Sarah (who was infertile and far beyond her childbearing years). Yet, because of His promise to Abraham, God miraculously allowed Sarah to become pregnant even at her advanced age, and she gave birth to Isaac, the promised son through whom God's new nation would descend.

Isaac married a woman named Rebecca, and they had twin sons named Esau and **Jacob.** Though Esau was older, Jacob conned him out of the birthright and blessing of their father, Isaac. In so doing, Jacob became the chosen individual through whom the promised nation would continue. By nature, Jacob was an intelligent, slick operator. He consistently manipulated and deceived others throughout his life. Yet, in spite of his flaws and shortcomings, Jacob expressed a real heart for God, and God continued to care for Jacob and work through him. Because of this, Jacob is a picture of *God's sovereign care*. During a defining moment in his life (Genesis 32), God changed Jacob's name to Israel. This is how the nation derived its permanent name.

Jacob (Israel) had twelve sons who became the original twelve tribes of the nation of Israel. The eleventh son, **Joseph**, being his father's favorite, was hated by his jealous brothers. In a tragic sequence of events, Joseph was betrayed by them and sold into slavery, winding up in Egypt. Surprisingly, Joseph landed on his feet and secured a good job with a decent employer. However, another unfortunate situation landed him in a political prison when he was framed for rape—a crime he didn't commit. Eventually, through the hand of God, Joseph caught a break. He was given a golden opportunity to impress the pharaoh of Egypt with an interpretation of two of the ruler's nightmares, which God enabled him to accurately interpret. Joseph was released from prison, put in charge of a famine-relief project, and promoted to second-in-command over the entire country of Egypt. Joseph's story is a picture of *God's sovereign control*, as God overrides the potentially devastating experiences woven into Joseph's life. In a moving story of forgiveness, Joseph eventually reconciled with his brothers and was reunited with his father. Due to the severity of the famine, Joseph relocated his entire extended family from Canaan to Egypt, including his father, Jacob (Israel).

This wraps up the book of Genesis. I try to remember the main thrust and the first two periods in the story of the Bible with the designation **"4x4"**—four major universal events: the **Creation,** the **Fall,** the **Flood,** and the **Tower of Babel,** plus the four major fathers of the faith: **Abraham, Isaac, Jacob,** and **Joseph.** One thing you'll notice in these stories is the fact that these are real people, struggling with the same kinds of situations and pressures we struggle with today. They had their faults, failures, and character flaws; yet, overriding those was an even bigger God, who had called each of these men to belong to Him. In the process, He continued to shape each of them for the role they would play in His plan to create *a common people.*

At the end of Genesis, the genetic nucleus of the nation of Israel was in place, living down in Egypt. This is where we pick up the next part of the story.

Plot Points: Genesis 12:1–9

Genesis 15:1–21

Genesis 25:19–34

Genesis 27:1–28:5

Genesis 32

Genesis 37

Genesis 39–41

Genesis 45

Chapter Three: Growing Up Tough

One of the darkest, yet most formative seasons in the life history of Israel was the period of **Egyptian Slavery and Exodus**. You can remember it by the **large "V"** in the napkin diagram. God had initiated the process of building a model nation—starting with the creation of a *common people* through the genetic line of Abraham. But the process of hardening them into a tightly knit people would be carried out and completed in the blast furnace of over four hundred years of oppression in Egypt. It was during this time that the essential identity of the nation was forged. The key figure in this section is a man named *Moses*. This part of the story is found in the opening chapters of the book of Exodus.

SLAVES IN EGYPT

After Joseph died, a new pharaoh rose to power in Egypt. Threatened by the rapid growth of the Hebrew people and fearing they would grow too strong and become a potential ally with Egypt's enemies, this pharaoh enslaved them, thus ushering in a season of suffering and oppression that lasted approximately four hundred years. In the process, the people of Israel lost touch with their God—the God of Abraham, Isaac, and Jacob. However, God never lost touch with them and never let go of them.

In Egypt, the Hebrew people multiplied rapidly. Eventually, another pharaoh came to power and instituted a program of mandatory infanticide upon the Hebrew people. Through a series of miraculous events, a Hebrew infant named Moses was secretly spared, adopted by the pharaoh's own daughter, and raised in the palaces of Egypt. For forty years, Moses was groomed for a future leadership role in Egypt. But one day, he murdered an Egyptian guard who was abusing a Hebrew slave, forcing him to flee into the wilderness of Sinai, where he became an obscure shepherd for the next forty years of his life.

But God had been preparing Moses all of his life for a monumental task: the deliverance of His people from their slavery in Egypt. In a dramatic encounter at a burning bush in the desert, Moses had a face-to-face experience with the God of his fathers, the Living and True God of Abraham, Isaac, and Jacob. The encounter changed everything for Moses. Persuaded by God, Moses returned to Egypt in an attempt to convince a new pharaoh to free the Israelites, allow them to leave Egypt, and migrate back to Canaan.

DELIVERANCE

Arriving back in Egypt, Moses discovered that the pharaoh was highly reluctant to grant Moses' request. So, using Moses as His vehicle, God unleashed a series of powerful plagues (each one intentionally aimed at exposing the powerlessness and inferiority of the Egyptian gods themselves), which finally convinced the pharaoh to let the Israelites leave. The entire nation left Egypt en masse—possibly one to two million strong. Soon afterward, the pharaoh caught a bad case of seller's remorse and went after them in order to bring them back. This set up the dramatic crossing of the Red Sea, where the Israelites, with their backs to the wall, were miraculously delivered by God's parting of the watery expanse separating Egypt from Saudi Arabia, known as the *yam suph*—the Sea of Reeds (or the Red Sea, as we know it). The Israelites passed through the Red Sea into the Sinai Peninsula. The pursuing Egyptian army was not so lucky. Just as its forces were crossing through in hot pursuit, the waters suddenly closed back on them and they were completely destroyed. The Israelite nation was rescued by God's miraculous, supernatural intervention. His people were now free to head toward their new home in Canaan.

Moses' life is a fascinating study in leadership. Imagine leading this many people through such physically demanding terrain with such Spartan physical, emotional, and spiritual resources, for forty years. It is simply one of the great leadership accomplishments of all time. His story unfolds in three forty-year periods. In the first forty years, he discovered the *emptiness of the world* in all that the Egyptian culture tried to offer him. During the next forty years as a shepherd, he discovered *who he was*. In the final forty years of leading the nation out of Egypt and through the wilderness toward Canaan, he discovered *who God was*.

It was during this period of slavery and deliverance that Israel was reintroduced to the God of their fathers, the God with whom they had lost touch during their slavery in Egypt. They were introduced to His reality, His identity, His matchless power, and His everlasting love for them as a people. Their deliverance from slavery in Egypt would forever be etched in their collective consciousness as the ultimate expression of God's saving power. They were finally, legitimately, a *common people*.

Now all they had to do was get back home to the land of Canaan, the land God had originally promised to Abraham. That little detail would prove harder and more difficult than they ever imagined.

Plot Points: Exodus 1–4
                   Exodus 7:1–6
                   Exodus 13:17–18
                   Exodus 14

Chapter Four: Take another Trip around Mount Sinai

It takes three elements to make up a legitimate nation: *a common people, a common code of conduct,* and *a common land.* The Israelites had become a common people in Egypt. As they stepped out into the wilderness of the Sinai Peninsula, they would receive a *common code of conduct*—a system of values and morals that would bind them even more closely together as a people.

POWER, PRESENCE, AND PROVISION

After crossing the Red Sea, approximately two million Israelites moved out into the Sinai Peninsula (present-day Saudi Arabia) and began to move south. Obviously, there was no way to pack enough food and water for a group that size on a trip of that magnitude on such short notice, so the people were completely dependent upon the miraculous provision of God for almost everything they needed. They had been "wowed" by God's *power* in Egypt, but now they would have a front-row seat in which to experience the *presence* and *provision* of God. This period in their national life is known as the *Wilderness Wanderings*. This season in the life of Israel is marked by the **wandering line on the right side of the "V"** in the diagram. During this time, they would be led by the literal presence of God in a pillar of cloud by day that turned luminescent at nightfall (a pillar of fire by night). God would provide the basic necessities of food through a supernatural, whole-food substance called manna; the occasional provision of quail; and water from the desert wadis (water was, on two occasions, miraculously provided from rock formations as well). God also provided spiritual leadership through Moses, his brother Aaron, sister Miriam, and Moses' understudy, a man named Joshua. God provided instructions for them to build a tabernacle (a sort of portable worship sanctuary) as well as instructions for the famous the Ark of the Covenant. But the most important thing God would provide for them would be the Law—the ceremonial and civil laws of the nation, anchored by the moral laws of the Ten Commandments.

A COMMON CODE OF CONDUCT

Moses camped out on the top of Mount Sinai for a period of forty days and there received the Ten Commandments—written by the very finger of God. The Ten Commandments, along with the rest of the civil and ceremonial law, provided the moral and organizational glue that would hold the nation together. But it did far more than that. It expressed not only the substantive character of God Himself but also how God had designed human beings and human life to operate at its optimum levels. It is impossible to communicate how revolutionary this development was for the Israelites and how central this Law would eventually become in their relationship with God. If human beings wanted to live in a relationship with God, they had to take on the commitment of living by God's Law— measuring up to all its rules and demands perfectly (the Israelites had a saying: "Do this and live!"). The Law would become the common code that would unite them as a geopolitical nation, and faithful obedience to it would enable them to experience a close relationship with God, too.

After receiving the Law (the Ten Commandments, as well as the civil and ceremonial laws), the nation began moving toward the promised land of Canaan. After two years in the wilderness, they finally reached its border, at a place called Kadesh Barnea. There, Moses sent twelve spies (including Joshua and another young leader named Caleb) into the land of Canaan to scope things out. The spies returned with a split report. All of the spies reported that the land was indeed a pretty amazing place, full of "milk and honey." Yet, all of them, except Joshua and Caleb, counseled Moses and the rest of the people not to move forward. They were afraid of the people in the land, the massively fortified cities, and the degree of difficulty that would be required to conquer the land. Only Joshua and Caleb counseled Moses and the people to trust God and move forward into their promised land.

But the damage was done. Freaked out for their own safety as well as the safety of their kids, the people balked.

ON THE ROAD AGAIN

In light of this lack of trust, God made a course correction with the nation. He led Israel to turn around and allowed them to continue wandering in the wilderness as a collection of nomadic tribes for the next 37½ years until all of the adult Israelites died off—all except for Joshua, Caleb, and Moses. During that time God continued to provide for His people and guide them. But that whole generation missed out on the future God had in store for them. They never saw or stepped foot in the land God had promised them. Even though Moses survived to the very end of that time, he was not allowed to enter the land either.

Forty years after they left Egypt, the nation arrived again at Kadesh Barnea—this time as a different community. The old generation had died off and the next generation had grown up, and they were sick of eating sand and manna. Needless to say, they were highly motivated to move forward into the land of Canaan and settle in permanently.

The wilderness wanderings are in many ways a parallel picture of our individual lives as people who belong to God. By the saving power of God, we've been rescued from slavery to the world system around us (symbolized in the culture of Egypt). We're headed for home, but we're not there yet. The journey is difficult, long, and sometimes filled with indecision, mistrust, false starts, glitches, and outright rebellion. Yet throughout the process we are learning and growing in our ability to follow God with greater devotion and sensitivity. We're not there yet—we haven't arrived, and our lives, though redeemed, are not fully complete, whole, or perfect yet. But we still belong to God. We have His power, His provision, His truth (His words), and His literal presence with us every step of the way. Someday, we will reach our final destination, because He has promised to get us there Himself.

The people of Israel visibly modeled these truths on the real-life stage of history. They had become a *common people*, held together by a *common code of conduct* and a faith in God. Now all they needed to become a legitimate nation was to settle in a *common land*—the land God had promised almost five hundred years earlier to Abraham.

Now it was time for them to unlock the door to their new home.

Plot Points: Exodus 19–20:21

Numbers 13–14

Deuteronomy 1:6–3:29,

Deuteronomy 7:1–10

Deuteronomy 34

Chapter Five: Crashing the Canaanites' Party

There was only one problem with moving right into the land of Canaan. Before the Israelites could settle there, they would have to drive out the various ethnic people-groups (collectively known as the Canaanites) who already lived in the land. The Canaanites were an advanced but extremely immoral and corrupt culture in the ancient world. Think of the Las Vegas strip on steroids. God was going to use His people, the Israelites, to execute final judgment on the Canaanites' extreme rebellion against Him. Extreme rebellion usually requires extreme measures. In this case, it would require their complete extermination. This era is known as the *Conquest of Canaan*, and is represented by the **"lightning bolts"** right after the large **"V"** on the diagram.

Moses brought this new version of the Hebrew nation up to Kadesh Barnea a second time. Most of this new generation hadn't seen the miracle of the rescue from Egypt, the crossing of the Red Sea, or the giving of the Ten Commandments. So while they were again camped at the edge of Canaan, Moses gave them a crash course in the Ten Commandments and the rest of the Old Testament Law (this crash course is called the book of Deuteronomy and comes from a contraction of two Greek words: *deuteron,* meaning "second," and *nomos,* meaning "law," thus the law given a second time). It was a reiteration and reinforcement of who they were as God's people and what God wanted them to do—especially as they got ready to enter the land of Canaan. When he had finished instructing the nation, Moses was given a glimpse of the land from the top of a mountain and then died before he had the chance to lead the people in. The nation was poised and ready to move into the land under the leadership of *Joshua,* who becomes the central character of the Bible's story at this point.

Through Moses, God commanded the nation of Israel to do three things when they entered the land: 1) totally wipe out the inhabitants of the land, 2) resist intermarrying with any of the people there (to maintain ethnic and religious purity), and 3) eradicate all traces of idolatry and Canaanite religion in the land (Deuteronomy 7:1–11). This was their mission, and these instructions were their marching orders.

Admittedly, this issue of the total extermination of an entire race of people and their culture naturally causes skeptics, seekers, and spiritual beginners to question the goodness of the God of the Bible. To totally wipe out a whole race of people—including innocent children and animals—not only sounds grossly unfair, it sounds downright wrong to our ears in this day and age. It doesn't seem to square with how a loving God is supposed to act. Why would God instruct the Israelites to do this to people who already lived in this land?

While the answer is more complex than the space we will devote to it here, one thing we must keep in mind is that the consequence of sin (living disconnected from God) is death. Death, in one or all of its forms (spiritual, emotional, psychological, and physical), is the natural penalty each one of us justly deserves—and justly deserves the very first time we sin and walk away from God. God has the perfect right to remove anyone or anything the first time they sin against Him or any time after that. It doesn't matter how it happens, when it happens, where it happens, or the means used. Death could come as a result of a car accident, a terminal disease, a tsunami, a natural disaster, war, famine, or old age.

Since the Canaanites were an unbelievably corrupt and evil society, God had every right to punch their ticket and terminate their lives at any time—the same right He has with any of us. For centuries, they had repeatedly thumbed their noses at God. They were engaged in the commission of unspeakable and destructive lifestyles that caused widespread harm to others around them. That He let them stick around as long as He did (or any of us, for that matter) is astonishing in and of itself. God had given them plenty of time to turn toward Him and turn things around. But they dug their heels in, continually refused to turn around, and, in doing so, made themselves irrevocable enemies of God—completely opposed to Him and everything He stood for. Since they repeatedly positioned themselves as His enemies, they were considered enemies of God's people, too. God was calling in their debt, and Israel was going to be His muscle to carry out the task. In addition to all of the other reasons above, God commanded the Israelites to do this so that they could establish themselves in the land as fully devoted followers of Him and not be contaminated by the practices of the Canaanite peoples.

The spiritual lesson for us is pretty clear. God's eventual agenda for this world is to completely eliminate every ounce of sin and evil in all its forms, as well as its consequences. He wants us to understand how destructive sin is, both to us and to others. This is the same agenda God has for our individual lives as well: to weed out all traces of sin and evil both inside us and around us. Is He committed to this process? Absolutely! In fact, He is even more committed to it than we are.

A COMMON LAND

The Old Testament book of Joshua records how the people of Israel skirted the southern border of Canaan, entered from the east across the Jordan River, and arrived at Jericho, where they won a stunning victory, thus splitting the Canaanite resistance in half. Following Joshua's lead, the Israelites moved south, defeating a southern coalition of Canaanite peoples. They then moved back north of Jericho, defeating a northern coalition of kings and their armies. This effectively broke the back of the Canaanite resistance. All of the major military victories were accomplished. From that point on, the people of Israel were expected to engage in a mop-up campaign. Joshua divided the land among the twelve tribes of Israel, with each tribe being responsible for clearing out any pockets of resistance from among the Canaanites in their respective territories. At the end of his life, Joshua issued a final challenge to the people, urging them to fully commit their lives to God, and themselves to finishing the job of driving out the Canaanites completely. The final chapter in the book of Joshua records Joshua's death.

At this point, Moses was gone and Joshua was gone. But the people of Israel had finally settled in, firmly entrenched in the *common land* God had promised to Abraham long ago. The final piece for the creation of God's model nation had finally been put in place.

Plot Points: Deuteronomy 4:1–14
                Deuteronomy 7:1–11
                Joshua 1:1–9
                Joshua 24:2–27

Chapter Six: 'Round and 'Round and 'Round She Goes…

The Israelites were finally home in the land God had promised to Abraham, Isaac, and Jacob. However, in the opening chapters of the book of Judges, we find that they bailed on the tasks God had given them. Once they settled in and secured the land, they failed to follow through completely on three essential tasks God gave them to accomplish: 1) they didn't completely wipe out all the inhabitants of the land, 2) they intermarried with the people there, and 3) they didn't destroy all the religious images and idols of the Canaanites. Yikes! This was not good.

Because they didn't follow through on their assigned responsibilities, the nation of Israel entered a **cyclical period,** known as the *Period of the Judges.* This period is represented by the **circular arrows** in the diagram. This vicious cycle consisted of four elements: 1) the Israelites' sin and failure to fully follow God, 2) harassment from one of the remaining people groups they'd failed to eliminate or one of their neighboring countries, 3) the Israelites' cry to God for help, and 4) God's deliverance through a charismatic leader, called a **judge**. While the names of many of these judges are unfamiliar to most of us, a few of them—Debra, Gideon, Barak, and Sampson—might ring a bell.

Each "judge" was a sort of hybrid between a military leader and a politician. When a neighboring nation oppressed one of the tribes of Israel, God would raise up a judge to throw off the oppressing nation and then restore some temporary peace and political stability to the oppressed territory or tribe. You have to remember that during this time, the nation of Israel was still a confederation of twelve tribes, loosely connected to each other, but largely operating independently—somewhat like the original thirteen colonies existed in the United States before the War of Revolution. The results of this system weren't pretty. This cycle of sin, oppression, crying out to God for help, and the sending of a judge to deliver His people, repeated itself at least a dozen times over and over again in the book of Judges. A spirit of moral/social/spiritual relativism permeated the nation of Israel. Twice in the book of Judges, we read the phrase defining the prevailing mood of the time: *"In those days, there was no king in Israel; everybody did that which was right in their own eyes"* (Judges 17:6; 21:25). Everybody did whatever they wanted or thought best for themselves at the time. Sounds sort of familiar, doesn't it?

One of the messages of this period is that if we're going to follow God, we've got to follow Him all the way and follow through completely on what He asks us to do. Following partially or half-heartedly is not optional. Otherwise, to the degree that we fail to do so, we find ourselves exposed to dangerous forces in the world around us—forces that will continue to harass, dominate, and control us. This is a consistent principle of spiritual life.

Israel floundered in this vicious cycle. There was no king in Israel. But with the final judge, a man named Samuel, all of that was about to change.

Plot Points: **Judges 1:19–2:23**
                   Judges 21:25

Chapter Seven: King Us!

When the people finally got fed up with the cycle of sin, oppression, crying out to God, and temporary deliverance through a judge, they came to Samuel, the final judge, and demanded a recall. They wanted change. No more temporary leaders. No more judges. They wanted a permanent leader—a king "like all the other nations have" (I Samuel 8:4–9).

As you might expect, Samuel was hurt by their demands at first. But God told him to give them what they wanted. By the way, it wasn't exactly wrong for them to want a king. In fact, during their wilderness wanderings, God had instructed Moses regarding what kind of king Israel should choose when one was finally anointed (Deuteronomy 17:14–20). The problem was that they wanted a king like all the other nations had—and that kind of king was *way* different than the kind of king God had in mind. As a final warning, and just so they knew what they were getting into, Samuel described what their kind of king would look like and how he would treat them. He then proceeded to find and anoint a king for them. The loose confederation of tribes was about to become a **unified kingdom**.

This **United Kingdom** period is marked by three major kings in succession: **Saul, David,** and **Solomon**—each reigning for approximately forty years over Israel. This period is represented in our diagram by **three large "spikes."** These three kings preside over an impressive "golden age" in the history of the nation of Israel, making her a major player in Middle Eastern world events. Some of the most memorable stories in the Bible take place during this United Kingdom era—stories about armies, battles, heroism, moral failures, palace intrigue, family betrayal, and world-class friendship.

Saul was the first king appointed over the nation of Israel. He was exactly what everyone was looking for. If Saul lived today, he would have won the People's Choice Award. If you were going to pick a king, Saul was Mr. Universe: handsome, big, strong, and in every way the most natural choice for king. That's why we mark Saul as the *fleshly choice* for king—the choice of our natural human instincts. Saul relied almost exclusively on his own natural charisma and personal strengths instead of relying on God. Eventually this approach cost him dearly. When Saul had simply wandered too far out and too far away from God, God removed Saul as king and gave the job to his understudy—a young shepherd/warrior named David.

David's life is a rags-to-riches story. The youngest of eight sons in his father's house, David fell into an almost freakish, once-in-a-lifetime opportunity, and he made the most of it. He took on—and won—a spectacular battle against a giant named Goliath, which launched him on a meteoric rise through the ranks of Saul's military leadership to become one of the top commanders of Israel's armies. Because David was so charismatic and gifted as a military leader, Saul soon began to feel threatened by him. In fact, Saul was so threatened that he made several attempts to have David eliminated. David was eventually forced to flee for his life. For a number of years, he lived as a fugitive, eluding Saul's search-and-destroy teams in the wilderness areas around southern Palestine. When Saul eventually died in battle, David returned and was crowned king over the nation.

What is most impressive about David was his heart for God. Because of this, we refer to David as *God's choice* for king. The nation of Israel grew into a world power under David, expanding its borders to the farthest dimensions in the nation's history. David unified the tribes, wrote a good portion of the Psalms in the Old Testament, and ushered in a period of unrivaled power and strength. He was the prototypical king God had desired for His nation, and he became the strongest king ever in its history. Because he sought God passionately, God promised David that his royal line would rule forever over the house of Israel (2 Samuel 7). This meant that someday the promised Messiah, who would ultimately reign permanently over the nation, would come from David's genetic line. This was quite a promise.

Though David failed God in many ways, as we all do, his heart was so soft toward God and so pro-God that, when he did fail, David quickly recognized it, turned around, and got back on track with God. On the basis of this kind of heart, God faithfully continued an intimate relationship with David throughout his life.

David's successor was his son **Solomon**, whose mother was the well-known Bathsheba. In spite of the fact that God blessed Solomon with wisdom far beyond his years, incredible wealth, a reign of peace and prosperity, and even gave him the honor of building the very first temple for God, Solomon was essentially a man of the world. On this basis, Solomon was the *worldly choice* for king. He did most of the things God had forbidden Israel's kings to do way back in Moses' day: things like multiply horses, multiply wealth, and multiply wives (he had seven hundred wives and three hundred concubines, most of them acquired in order to solidify political alliances with neighboring countries). Eventually, Solomon's foreign wives turned his heart away from God. Solomon is the picture of a person with a divided heart. As a result of his divided loyalty, God split Solomon's kingdom into two kingdoms after his death in 931 BCE.

The United Kingdom period teaches us an important lesson about spiritual commitment to God: ninety-five percent devotion to God is still five percent short—and even five percent non-devotion can come back to bite us. Because Solomon was a divided man with a divided heart, the United Kingdom fractured and splintered after his death, becoming a house divided against itself.

Plot Points: 1 Samuel 8

1 Samuel 15:1–16:12

2 Samuel 7

1 Kings 1:28–37

1 Kings 10:23–11:13

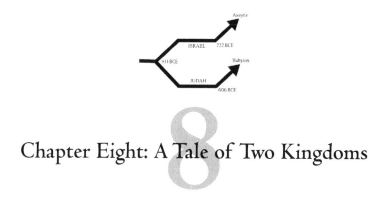

Chapter Eight: A Tale of Two Kingdoms

With the death of Solomon, a messy period of disunity, schism, and division enveloped the nation of Israel until, eventually, the wheels of God's model nation came off. This period of the nation's history is the tragic story of the **Divided Kingdom,** indicated by the **split parallel lines** on our diagram.

Solomon's successor, his son Rehoboam, was disliked by a large percentage of the populace. In light of this, Rehoboam's jealous brother Jereboam carried out a military coup that split the kingdom in two, with ten of the northern tribes forming a **northern kingdom calling itself Israel,** seceding from the two remaining southern tribes, Benjamin and Judah. These two southern tribes then banded together to form **a southern kingdom called Judah.** The story of these two sibling kingdoms takes up most of the story in the Old Testament books of 1 and 2 Kings, as well as 1 and 2 Chronicles, and forms the background for almost all of the major and minor prophetic books in the rest of the Old Testament. As you read through this section, keep in mind that often the stories of the northern kingdom of Israel and the southern kingdom of Judah alternate back and forth in the texts. It keeps you on your toes as you read!

THE NORTHERN KINGDOM, ISRAEL

All you need to know about the northern kingdom of Israel is that it was a complete train wreck. They had nineteen kings—all of them evil. They abandoned the true worship of God, starting their own religion by blending forms of pagan worship with some traditional Hebrew worship elements to form a hybrid religious system. They thought this would give them their own unique identity as a nation and enable them to compete with the spiritually conservative religion of the southern kingdom, Judah. This northern kingdom of Israel became an incorrigibly corrupt nation whose leaders abused the common people. Because of this, God put the hammer down on them. In 722 BCE, He allowed them to be overrun and conquered by a new world power, Assyria. Assyria was a brutal nation that almost completely wiped out the ten tribes of the northern kingdom, absorbing them into the Assyrian Empire through a program of forced relocation and eventual assimilation. This northern kingdom was effectually never heard from again. Their fall is indicated by the **sharp diagonal trajectory of the upper line** on our diagram.

THE SOUTHERN KINGDOM, JUDAH

Parallel to the story of the northern kingdom of Israel is the story of the southern kingdom, Judah. It was a little better than the northern kingdom, but not by much. While this kingdom also had nineteen kings (and one queen mother), these rulers exercised both good and evil reigns in a kind of alternating and random pattern. When things were good, they were very, very good, but when things were bad—they were horrid! Eventually, the nation of Judah also spiraled downward until God dropped the hammer on them, too. In 606 BCE, the Babylonians (the newest bully on the geopolitical block) invaded Judah, leveling the walls of Jerusalem, deporting the brightest and best of the population to Babylon (the name of Daniel might ring a bell here for some people), plundering the city, and destroying the temple. There is no other way to say it: The nation of Judah just got *crushed*. Her people were beaten down, enslaved, and a portion of the population driven into forced exile to Babylon for seventy years. The demise of the kingdom of Judah is pictured by **the sharp upward diagonal trajectory of the lower line** of our diagram.

SENDING IN THE PROPHETS

This period of the divided kingdom was also the great period of the prophets. This was the era when God repeatedly tried to speak to both nations using the voices of various men like Elijah, Isaiah, Jeremiah, Ezekiel, Habakkuk, and others of what are sometimes called the major and minor prophets. These divine spokesmen were God's **megaphone** to the kings of the nations and to the people as well—calling them to turn back to God and predicting an ugly future for them if they did not. Sometimes these prophets acted as God's "two-by-fours"—a confrontational presence designed to get the leaders' attention through miracles and predictive prophecy. At other times, they simply spoke God's truth clearly and directly to the nation and its leaders, calling them to repent and turn back to God. Like most whistle-blowers, they were famously unpopular—especially with those at the top of the social/political/religious food chain. But through them, we see God patiently reaching out time and time again to His people, giving them opportunity after opportunity to turn things around and get them right. Sadly, neither nation was able to do so.

In spite of their horrendous failures, God wasn't finished with His people yet. It was also the prophets who predicted that after their captivity in Babylon, some of the people (a "remnant") from the southern kingdom of Judah would return to their land. It was these same prophets who continued to whisper hope into the ear of the nation, reminding them that God still had a future for them. The Babylonian exile would in fact become another defining moment in the collective life of the Jewish people. They would learn profound lessons through this difficult time.

The learning curve would be steep.

Plot Points: **2 Kings 17:1–23**

                     2 Chronicles 36:11–21

Chapter Nine: To Babylon and Back

For seventy years, the survivors of the nation of Judah lived in relocation camps around the city of Babylon. You might expect their captivity would have severely traumatized and weakened them. But again, the grace of God was at work protecting them, even when they didn't always realize it. Segregated from the Babylonian populace into a sort of "ghetto" situation, very little ethnic assimilation occurred. The Jewish people were allowed limited travel opportunities, were able to own and operate businesses, and, interestingly enough were pretty much left to themselves.

Some other developments also took place during this time period. The general populace of the nation lost their ability to read, write, and even speak the Hebrew language, adopting Aramaic as their common tongue. However, to keep their faith alive and vital without a temple in which to offer sacrifices, they started something called the synagogue— small gatherings where they could at least read from the Old Testament Law and prophetic writings in Hebrew (the Old Testament writings had not yet been collected and preserved as a single entity). The Israelites, who up to this point had been a people of the temple, slowly became a people of the Scriptures—a people fiercely committed to the centrality of God's Law in their lives. Instead of the rituals and sacrifices revolving around Temple worship, the Old Testament writings and commandments became the pivotal object of their faith.

This state of affairs had a revolutionary effect on the people of Israel. From this point on, we never again see the nation of Israel turn back to worship idols or engage in pagan religious practices of any kind. God had used these circumstances to purify them as a nation without their realizing it. In the process, He was laying the groundwork to bring them back to their land—the land of Israel.

After seventy years in exile, Babylon was defeated by the new world power, Media-Persia. Under the Median-Persian kings Cyrus and Artexerxes, the people of Israel were allowed to **return** to Israel to **rebuild** their nation. This movement is designated by **the downward arrow** in our diagram. It is often an era referred to as the **Babylonian Captivity and Return.**

There were three major returns for the rebuilding of the nation of Israel: 1) a return under the leadership of a man named **Zerubbabel** to *rebuild the temple*, 2) another return under the leadership of a scribe named **Ezra** in order to *rebuild the people,* and 3) a final return under **Nehemiah** in order to *rebuild the walls of Jerusalem.* God made good on His promises through the prophets to bring His people back to their land again in order to serve Him there. Three prophets who spoke to and encouraged the people during this time were Haggai, Zechariah, and Malachi.

With the book of Malachi, the Old Testament ends on a somewhat minor chord. While the people are back in the land, the temple rebuilt, and the city secure, there was nevertheless a restless, unfinished feel to the story. The Jewish people were still a stubborn people who, in spite of their best intentions, continued to ignore, neglect, and forget God. Though back in their land, their existence was marked by continued servitude to foreign nations, unfulfilled longings, suspended hopes, and unrealized promises. It would be almost four hundred years before they would definitively see God move among them again.

But when He did move, He pulled back the curtain on the central act of the biblical story—the watershed event of all of human history.

Though they didn't know it yet, Christmas was coming. First, though, the stage had to be set and all props had to be put in place.

Plot Points: Ezra 1:1–6

Ezra 7:1–10

Nehemiah 1:1–2:18

Nehemiah 6:15–16

Chapter Ten: Setting the Stage

From the time of Malachi (the final book in the Old Testament) until the beginning of the New Testament book of Matthew, there elapses a period of almost four hundred years of biblical silence from God. These four centuries, known as the **Inter-Testamental Period**, are indicated by, well, not much, except **three dots** in our diagram. No major prophets emerged, no inspired books of the Bible were penned, no defining moments of relevant spiritual history were recorded, no direct revelations from God were written down. It was like a giant pause in the flow of the story—like the pooling eddy of a river. Don't get the wrong idea. Just because God didn't "speak" or act in recorded biblical ways didn't mean He wasn't around and active in the world. On the contrary, God was still very much engaged, working behind the scenes to position the entire then-known world for the grandest entrance in human history and the centerpiece of the whole story of the Bible, the coming of the promised Messiah. This was a highly formative period not only for the nation of Israel, but for the entire world as well.

Galatians 4:4 tells us, *"But when the **time had fully come**, God sent His Son, born of a woman, born under law, to redeem those under law, that we might receive the full rights of sons."* God was in the process of setting the stage for Messiah's entrance. During this waiting period, God positioned the world for His arrival through five major socio-historical developments.

1) **The Spread of the Greek Language**: During the fourth century BCE, Alexander the Great and his armies were running around conquering the then-known ancient world. In the process, Greek culture and language spread throughout the Alexandrian Empire, and Greek became the official trade language of the empire—much like English is today. This development was highly advantageous for the spread of culture, education, and new ideas—which would be greatly facilitated by having a common language known to all.

2) **The Spread of Roman Law and *Pax Romana***: Following Greece, Rome became the next dominant world empire, uniting the Mediterranean world through a network of highways that provided unrestricted trade and safe, secure travel under the *Pax Romana* (the "Roman peace"). This, in effect, shrank the world. Freedom of movement throughout the ancient world allowed cultural practices and new religious ideas to co-mingle and spread into every major urban center of the ancient world.

3) **The Development of the Synagogue**: As we mentioned earlier, during the Babylonian captivity, the people of Israel adjusted the core practices of their faith away from the rituals and sacrifices of the temple (sometimes called the *"cultus"* by religious scholars) to a religious life without a temple (and thus no rituals or sacrifices). They developed the synagogue, which revolved primarily around the reading the Old Testament Law and the

promotion of strict adherence to its directives. Thereafter, wherever the Jews eventually moved around the world, they would start synagogues to facilitate the practice of their faith. How cool was it that when early Jewish Christians began sharing the discovery of their promised Messiah, they had such a natural place to gain a hearing in almost every city in the Roman Empire? Talk about strategic!

4) **Universal Moral Degeneration:** The entire moral fabric of the Greek and Roman society was shredded. Sure, there was widespread religious diversity in the empire, but there were also huge holes in people's souls. The masses were hungry for something real in which to believe. God allowed the natural consequences of sin, the inferior quality of spiritual alternatives, and the breakdown of social/moral structures to prepare a fertile soil for the arrival of Messiah.

5) **The Widespread Practice of Slavery:** It's estimated that by the end of the first century BCE, almost fifty to sixty percent of the population of the Roman Empire were slaves. This meant that almost half the empire was comprised of those who were poor, oppressed, and marginalized, and thus would provide a highly receptive environment in which to speak the message of new life, new hope, and inner freedom that would be found in the arrival of Messiah.

These five developments shaped the moral and spiritual texture of the ancient world. When all these factors converged, the world was unknowingly positioned for the entrance of the Messiah—that singular human representative who would come and crush the power of sin and evil forever. That One who'd been promised all the way back in Genesis 3:15—toward whom all of the Old Testament Law, the prophets, the symbols, the rituals, the institutions, and the Scriptures pointed—was about to arrive.

At last, we come to the main event. The Star of the story is ready to take center stage.

Chapter Eleven: God with Us

What is the greatest moment in human history? If we conducted a survey, we'd no doubt compile a variety of answers. But if we asked, "What is the greatest moment in *spiritual* history?" religious historians, scholars, and even a large percentage of people around the globe would offer a resounding consensus: the birth of Jesus of Nazareth. There is simply no person in all of human history who has affected our world the way He has affected it. The Bible boldly and unequivocally declares that this Jesus was in fact the Messiah promised by God from long ago. He is the main character of the biblical story, and His entrance to center stage is pictured by the **large cross** in our diagram. Today, we celebrate His birth at Christmas, and virtually the whole world takes a timeout. Indeed, His life remains the greatest one ever lived on our planet. In Jesus, the Living and True God of the Universe packaged Himself in human flesh and came personally—to us and for us. In doing so, He entered our world, lived on our turf, and gave us the clearest picture of God we will ever have.

No wonder we call him Savior, Messiah, Immanuel ("God with us").

The first four books of the New Testament portion of the Bible are the historic, insider accounts of the life and works of Jesus Christ, written by those who knew Him best. While these four accounts are incredibly similar in many details, they are also unique from one another—each one giving us a valid and consistent, yet slightly different, angle on the person and work of Jesus. Some scholars struggle with the differences in style, chronology, and peripheral details among these four accounts. However, despite the minor stylistic differences these accounts display, they are amazingly consistent and are without contradiction regarding the essential identity and message of Jesus.

Though this is difficult for us to wrap our heads around, it may help to think about the alleged "discrepancies" this way. Suppose I asked four people—the painter Vincent Van Gogh, the music group Cold Play, writer Walt Whitman, and talk-show host Oprah Winfrey—to give a description of a specific event, say, the same sunset on the same day. I think it would be safe to say that their recollections and renderings of that same sunset would be unique and different from each other, yet still very accurate regarding the event itself according to each communicator's medium and perspective. Each source might add or subtract certain aspects of the event or describe them in terms that would enrich the others in complementary kinds of ways. In a sense, that's what we have in the four gospels: four primary source documents, written either by eyewitnesses themselves or close acquaintances of those who were eyewitnesses to the events—and all written within a generation of Jesus' life and ministry. I like to call these four insider accounts the **Four Faces of Jesus.**

Matthew presents Jesus as the fulfillment of the *Jewish Messiah*, Mark presents Jesus as the *Ultimate Servant*, Luke focuses on Jesus' *Perfect Humanity*, and John focuses on Jesus' inner identity as *God Himself* in the flesh. These four "gospels" (accounts of the good news) are considered our most historically reliable accounts of Jesus' life by an overwhelming majority of scholars. There are no other historical records on the planet that even come close to possessing the accuracy and reliability level these four possess.

The gospel accounts trace the life of Jesus through the crucial movements of His earthly life: His birth, His baptism by John the Baptist and His introduction into public ministry, His temptation, His three-plus years of ministry from age thirty covering His miraculous works, His teachings, and His interactions with people on a very personal level. But head-and-shoulders above these previous moments stand the monumental events surrounding His voluntary crucifixion for the sins of the human race, His resurrection from the dead, and His ascension into heaven (His physical departure from this planet, but not the cessation of His presence in the world). These events form the fundamental defining moments of Jesus' life. Fully ninety percent of these four gospel accounts focus on the three years of Jesus' public ministry, with each account giving special emphasis to the final week of His life.

The New Testament tells us that Jesus was one hundred percent human. He was our fully human representative, living a perfect human life, thus demonstrating for us how a real human being functions in a right relationship with God. But He was also beyond human. The people who knew Him intimately also recognized (as Jesus Himself directly claimed) that He was one hundred percent God. This Jesus was in fact the Maker and Creator of the universe, packaged in human flesh, displaying the exact inner attributes and essential nature of God, and demonstrating what God was like in a precise, concrete, and ultra-personal way. Robert Oppenheimer, one of the developers of the atomic bomb, once said that if you really want to communicate an idea, you should wrap it in a person. This is what God did. In becoming human, He wrapped Himself in the person of Jesus of Nazareth, thus clearly communicating who He was and what He was like.

Jesus' coming, then, was highly strategic. He came to teach us about God, to teach us about ourselves, and to offer us a way to recover our full potential as human beings through a fresh relational connection with God. His message was that God was offering a new way of life to all who would embrace Jesus Himself as the personal leader of their entire lives—for the rest of their lives. This reconnection with God would not happen by trying harder to be a better person, behavior modification, doing more for God, or simply agreeing intellectually with a list of statements about God. This renewed connection with God could only happen by embracing Jesus Himself and entering into a whole-life partnership with Him. On the cross, Jesus died in our place, making the full payment for the death penalty demanded by our sins. On the cross, Jesus became the forgiver of humanity's sins. On the cross, Jesus took our place, and absorbed all the brutality, violence, and hatred that the punishment for sin and evil deserved—and He did this on behalf of all people, for all of time. He was the singular human representative whom God promised long ago—the One who would conquer the power of sin, evil, and death forever.

That's not the end of the story. Three days after His execution, the brutalized body of Jesus was brought back to life by the power of the living God. His grave was empty. His disciples claimed that He physically appeared to them, and not just to one or two of them, but to all of them, and even others beyond that inner circle. The Roman and Jewish authorities had no answer for this, could not produce a body, and had little choice but to try to cover it up and spin it as best they could. But one of the most well-attested, historical facts of the ancient world would simply not go away. Jesus had been resurrected from the dead, never to die again. He had conquered both the power of sin and the power of death forever.

This is the good news of the Christian faith. Jesus is living—right here, right now, in this world, for this life, and for all time. Because He is alive now, He is able to become the **personal leader** of an individual's life. In Him, we discover the One who was designed to complete our lives as human beings. Through His resurrected life living in us, we can draw on the internal power He provides in order to progressively overcome the *power* and the *presence* of sin in our daily lives. His internal presence enables us to live the kind of lives He designed us to live. This is the difference Jesus makes: not just to save people *from* their sin, but to save them *for* a different quality of life, a life that never quits, fades, or ends—an indestructible quality of life. This life can begin for anybody, right here, right now, in this lifetime, extending forever into eternity. When you lock into this life, it reorders your entire world: your mind, your heart, your actions, your drives, your behavior, your relationships, your priorities—it reorders everything around Jesus.

This is the outrageous, almost ridiculous message of Christianity. What men and women in the past could not do for themselves by worshipping lesser gods, by trying to measure up to manmade codes of conduct, or even by trying to keep the demands of the Old Testament Law, Jesus accomplished for us in His death and resurrection. What we cannot do today through religious activity, self-help seminars, self-improvement programs, or behavior modification, God has already done for us in Jesus Christ. For every person on the planet, Jesus offers the possibility of a new relationship with God through a new relationship with Jesus Himself. He is the only one who can offer this to us because He is the only One in all of life who is both God and man.

If there is anything we should realize about God by now, it's that He's not going to be satisfied with rescuing just a select few. He wants to bring as many people as possible back home into His new spiritual family. Like a great river spreading out into a massive delta area, God wanted His influence to spread out and affect an entire world. His great dream to bring all the nations of the earth back together again was just beginning. Jesus' ragtag group of followers would become an army of storytellers to the rest of the world. This is what the next bend in the great story of God is all about.

Plot Points: John 1:1–18

                   I Corinthians 15:3–8

Chapter Twelve: Jesus Reloaded (In His Church)

After His resurrection, Jesus remained here on earth for a brief time, meeting regularly with His followers until He physically ascended once and for all into the heavens. But His ministry didn't stop with His physical departure from this earth. The rest of the story is that He's still alive and working in our world today. He still speaks, still heals, still works miracles, still changes the lives and eternal trajectories of lost, disconnected people. He has a voice, arms, hands, and feet. But He is no longer contained in nor limited to a singular human body. Instead, He has a different kind of "body." Jesus' physical, resurrected life is now "reloaded" in those people who have embraced Him, belong to Him, and have been infected with His life—that grouping of followers called "the Church." In the New Testament, the Church is not conceived of as an institution, an organization, or a building; it is positioned as the collection of people of each gender, in every generation, from every nationality, throughout all time, in all periods of human history, who have ever become, or ever will become, followers of Jesus. We call this new entity the "Big C" Church—the Church universal, the body of Christ.

The story of its birth and growth is found in the book of Acts and then fleshed out in more detail in some of the other writings that make up the rest of the New Testament.

During His earthly ministry, Jesus had promised His followers He would create a new community of people called the Church. In the New Testament book of Acts, He explained to His disciples that He would personally indwell them and live His life and His message through them both individually and collectively. Like an invading army, they would storm the very gates of hell itself, rescuing people imprisoned by sin, evil, oppression, exploitation, and trauma. Jesus taught that the kingdom of evil and darkness, embedded in the world order and the human systems all around us, would not be able to withstand their powerful advance. The book of Acts (the story of the spiritual activities, or "acts," of his early followers) tells this part of the story—the story of the birth, expansion, and continuation of Jesus' ministry through the Church. My personal title for this spiritual movement is *Jesus Reloaded.*

Actually, Acts 1:8 says it all. These followers, indwelt and empowered by the Holy Spirit of God, took His message to the world. They started in Jerusalem, expanded into Judea (the region around Jerusalem), moved into Samaria (a territory inhabited by an ethnic group that was half-Jewish, half non-Jewish), and then finally reached out into the most remote corners of the earth. This geographic spread of the Church is represented by **the four spreading lines after the cross of Jesus** in our diagram. They picture this four-fold expansion of the movement—first in Jerusalem, and then into Judea, Samaria, and, ultimately, to the utter-most parts of the earth. Essentially, the mission of this new community of followers was to spread the message here, there, and everywhere.

The book of Acts chronicles the attempts of Jesus' followers to do exactly that. His Church, under the leadership of men like Peter, John, James, Philip, the Apostle Paul, and others, brought the message of new life and new hope in Jesus to the outer limits of the Roman Empire within fifty years of the death and resurrection of Jesus. In the wake of this exponential growth, the course of human history and of Western civilization would forever be altered.

The book of Acts closes somewhat open-ended, with the Apostle Paul under house arrest in the city of Rome, awaiting trial for his faith. Such a clipped ending inevitably leaves us hanging a bit, left with the impression that there's still more to come, that the story somehow wasn't finished. Indeed, it wasn't—not by a long shot. In a weird sort of way, spiritual history continued to be written through the ages. It continues to be written even today, as Jesus is still reaching out to new people, in new locations, and to new people-groups around the world through His body, the Church.

Almost all the rest of the New Testament writings were penned by leaders of that first-century Church to local churches or individuals in various cities throughout the Roman Empire. They were designed to give an accurate interpretation and application of Jesus' life and work to everyday situations that His followers faced—both inside and outside the Church. How else would these new believers know what to believe and how to live out their newfound faith in the trenches of everyday life? These New Testament letters were circulated among the churches, collected, and eventually subjected to rigorous evaluation of their content and historicity by the Councils of Hippo and Carthage. They were then preserved in order to inform and encourage Jesus' followers not only in their own day, but also for future generations of Christ-followers in the centuries to come. Someone once told me that the Bible is God's love letter to us; to get the message personally, we need to read between the lines. Nowhere is this dynamic more evident than in these personal letters where we read directly as well as between the lines about God's desires and dreams for those who belong to Him.

Thus we come to the end of the story. The book of Revelation closes out the Bible by describing some of the forces and events that will surround the end of human history as we know it. Jesus promised His disciples both before and after His death that He would someday personally return again to this earth. He promised them that when that moment ultimately arrived, He would wrap up human history, clean up the mess we'd made of things, set everything right, and usher in eternity for those who belong to Him. In cryptic fashion, using wild, surrealistic images, couched in a writing style known as apocalyptic literature, the book of Revelation conveys the story of God closing the door on this world and opening the door to the next.

Of course, this was God's plan all along. From the third chapter of Genesis to the twenty-second chapter of Revelation, God has been, is, and always will be about the business of searching for and finding lost, disconnected people in order to win their hearts back and bring them home to be with Him again forever. This is His mission, focus, and goal. And He could not be more committed to its fulfillment.

Karl Barth, a great biblical scholar, was once asked what he considered the most profound theological truth he had ever encountered. He responded, "Jesus loves me, this I know, for the Bible tells me so." This book, the Bible, is the story of God's constant, relentless pursuit of mankind. It is the story of Jesus coming after us in order to win us back with an irrational, outrageous, never-ending, life-changing love.

Plot Points: Acts 1–2 (especially 1:8)

2 Peter 3:1–13

Revelation 1

Revelation 21–22

Chapter Thirteen: You and the Great Story of God

The great martial-arts expert Bruce Lee was not just a great fighter; he was also a philosopher of sorts. He explained his philosophy about life and his craft in a this way: "You put water into a cup, it becomes the cup. You put water into a bottle, it becomes the bottle. You put it in a teapot, it becomes a teapot. The water can flow. The water can crash. Be water, my friend."[1]

This book, the Bible, is water—liquid. In places it is swift and powerful, while in others it is quiet and soothing. Sometimes it hits us with sledge-hammer force, rocking our thoughts, confronting our behavior, and pushing us away from disaster. Sometimes it is gentle and comforting, washing over us, refreshing us, and cleansing our bodies and souls. It moves us, awakens us, fills us, satisfies us. Give it enough time and it will move mountains, cut holes in rocks, or make a desert bloom. It is powerful and alive and fluid, able to find its way into the deepest holes of the human heart.

This story of God somehow has this ability to adapt itself, speaking to every time and culture, to every person in every place and time, across the generations. It often changes course, flowing around cultural, social, and personal obstacles, yet it does so without changing its essential message. Its current carries us with its wisdom, insight, inspiration, and direction.

One of the beautiful facets of the Bible is that it contains *our* story too. The Bible is not just about other people in other times and places. It's my story. It's your story, too. When we read the Bible, we somehow find ourselves in it. I like the way Rob Bell puts it in his book *Velvet Elvis*: "The Bible tells a story—a story that isn't over yet, a story that is still being told, a story in which we still play a part ... these stories [in the Bible] are our stories. They are alive and active and teaching us about our lives in our world today. These stories still work on us. We start out reading them, but they end up reading us."[2] When we read about Adam turning away from God in the Garden of Eden, we instantly relate to him because we've also turned away from God in our own lives. When God's people are ticked off at Him for leading them out into the desolation of the wilderness, that's the way we feel sometimes when God leads us in unexpected ways. When we watch Jesus' followers struggle to believe in Him even after His resurrection, their questions and doubts are the same questions and doubts we struggle with. We are there in the stories – because they are essentially our stories too.

Willa Cather, a nineteenth-century journalist, once wrote, "There are only two or three human stories and they go on repeating themselves as fiercely as if they had never happened before."[3] And the beat goes on.

I have come to the conclusion that we, as human beings, are either rut stories or river stories. We are either people stuck in the same old channels, thinking the same thoughts, doing the same stuff, making the same tragic errors and mistakes as everyone before and after us, our lives slowly accumulating algae and becoming cloudier and more toxic by the day. Or we are river stories, caught up in the current of God and His activity in human history, brimming with life and vitality, moving in fresh, new ways, expanding our capacities, shaping the landscape around us, and bringing life to all we come in contact with.

I hope that as you've read this book, somewhere along the line, you will have seen yourself in this grand, sweeping, epic story that is the great story of God. You are in here somewhere. Maybe as you read this book, you've realized that your life is a "rut" story. If so, why not take some time to stop and reflect? Ask yourself, "What's keeping me here? What do I really want for my life? Do I really want to just continue in the same old paths and patterns that are not working for me?" What would it take for you to move out into the middle and become a 'river' story? Jesus told us how to do this. Think differently about God, life, and the world. Ditch your old way of living, turn around, and embrace Him and this new way of life found in Him.

If you are not at this point yet in your spiritual journey, may I make a suggestion? Keep searching. Investigate and explore the Bible. Read it firsthand and evaluate for yourself who Jesus is and what He offers to you. My prayer for you is that someday you will make the decision to give yourself to this Jesus with all you have and all that you are. When you do that, I hope that you will keep reading this story, the Bible, over and over and over again, discovering fresh, new insights that will help you understand Jesus better, highlight Him with greater clarity, make Him more real to you, and inspire you to follow Him more fully with your life. Finally, I pray you will become an active and committed part of the movement of His followers—the Church of Jesus—using your time, talents, and treasures to carry the message about Jesus to a world literally dying to live.

"The only two things that can satisfy the human soul," English writer G.K. Chesterton observes, "are a person, and a story—and even a story must be about a person."[4] This Jesus—the promised Messiah, the One who is the Maker, Creator, Sustainer, and Redeemer of human life—He is the story, the whole story. He alone is the one true Hope for our lives—and the one true Hope for our world.

The Liquid Bible Remixed

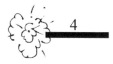

The Primeval Period

Beginnings: Four Universal Events—Creation, Fall, Flood, Tower of Babel

Emphasis: God's universal interactions with broken, lost people

The Four Fathers Period

God begins to create a model nation and a magnet nation to attract the
scattered nations of the world and lead them back to Him.

He accomplishes this through the Four Fathers of the Faith: Abraham,
Isaac, Jacob, and Joseph.

The Egyptian Slavery Period

Joseph becomes the second most powerful man in Egypt.

Joseph relocates his father, Jacob, and his eleven brothers and their families to Egypt.

A new Egyptian king comes to power and enslaves the Israelites for four
hundred-plus years.

Moses is raised up to lead the people out of Egypt—which he does.

The Exodus/Wilderness Wanderings Period

The Israelites escape into the desert, receive the Ten Commandments
along with the civil and ceremonial laws, prepare to enter the promised land, balk, and then wander in the wilderness of the Sinai Peninsula for a grand total of forty years.

The Conquest Period

Joshua leads the people into the promised land of Canaan, conquers the
   nations living there, and divvies up the land among the twelve tribes
   of Israel.

The Judges Period

Once settled in the land, Israel fails to comply with God's directives to
   completely destroy the Canaanites.

Israel falls into a cycle of sin/oppression from her neighboring enemies/
   crying out to God/temporary deliverance through a "judge."

The prevailing attitude: moral relativism, chaos, and disunity

The United Kingdom Period

The People of Israel are tired of the "judges" system of government and
   ask Samuel for a king.

This period revolves around three kings who unified Israel: Saul, David,
   and Solomon.

Because of Solomon's divided heart, God divides the kingdom after Solomon's death in 931 BCE.

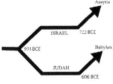

The Divided Kingdom Period

The kingdom splits into two kingdoms: a northern kingdom (Israel) and
   a southern kingdom (Judah).

Israel is totally corrupt and is utterly destroyed by the Assyrians in 722
   BCE.

Judah lasts a little longer but is eventually conquered by Babylon circa 606 BCE.

Jerusalem and its walls are torn down, the temple leveled, and many of the people deported to Babylon for seventy years.

The Captivity and Exile Period

People of Israel spend seventy years as refugees in exile in Babylon.

The nation becomes a people of the law instead of the Temple.

The Return/Rebuilding Period

Babylon is conquered by a new world power, Media-Persia.

Under Cyrus, the people of Judah are allowed to return to their land.

Three separate returns occur: one under Zerubbabel to rebuild the temple, one under Ezra to rebuild the people, and a final one under Nehemiah to rebuild the walls of Jerusalem.

Setting The Stage (Inter-Testamental Period)   ● ● ●

There is a period of approximately four hundred years between the end of the Old Testament and the beginning of the New Testament.

Meanwhile, God is at work, secretly preparing the world for the coming of Messiah.

God with Us (The Life and Ministry of Jesus Period)

Jesus comes to our world, lives the greatest life ever lived, engages in a public ministry of three-plus years, is crucified for the sins of the world, and rises from the dead three days later.

Jesus Reloaded (The Beginning and Growth of Jesus' Church)

Jesus continues to live in and work through His new "body," the Church.

The Church begins in Jerusalem, spreads to Judea, then Samaria, and eventually to the ends of the earth.

We live in this period of time right now as Jesus continues to work through the collective life of His people, who make up the Church.

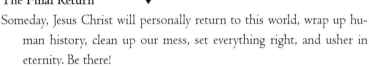

The Final Return

Someday, Jesus Christ will personally return to this world, wrap up human history, clean up our mess, set everything right, and usher in eternity. Be there!

Notes

1 Dave Gibbons, *The Monkey and the Fish* (Zondervan, Grand Rapids, 2009), pp. 92–93

2 Rob Bell, *Velvet Elvis* (Zondervan, Grand Rapids, 2005), pp. 66, 60

3 Willa Cather, from Steven B. Sample, *The Contrarian's Guide to Leadership* (Wiley, San Francisco, 2002), p. 58

4 G.K. Chesterton, source unknown

Bibliography

All Scripture quotations/scriptural allusions from *The Holy Bible, New International Version*, International Bible Society, Zondervan, Grand Rapids, 1984

A History of Israel, John Bright, The Westminster Press, Philadelphia, 1976

A Survey of Israel's History, Leon Wood, Zondervan Press, Grand Rapids, 1970

A Survey of Old Testament Introduction, Gleason Archer, Moody Press, Chicago, 1978

Bible History, Old Testament, Alfred Edershiem, William B. Eerdmans Publishing Co., Grand Rapids, 1975

Introduction to the Old Testament, Roland Kenneth Harrison, William B. Eerdmans Publishing Co., Grand Rapids, 1969

The Contrarian's Guide to Leadership, Steven B. Sample, Wiley Press, San Francisco, 2002

The Greek New Testament, 4th *Revised Edition*, United Bible Societies, USA, Stuttgart, 1983

The Monkey and the Fish, Dave Gibbons, Zondervan, Grand Rapids, 2009

Velvet Elvis, Rob Bell, Zondervan, Grand Rapids, 2005

About the Author

Paul Thome attended Western Seminary and graduated from Peninsula Bible Church's Scribe School. He has been a local church pastor for over twenty-eight years and currently serves as the Pastor of Spiritual Formation and Leadership Development at Sun River Church in Rancho Cordova, California. In addition, he is an adjunct professor at Western Seminary's Sacramento Campus, an ACC Certified Personal and Professional Coach, and founder  of *LEDR Coaching and Training*, which provides personal coaching services, as well as offering training seminars for local churches, missionary and para-church organizations, and other corporate organizations.

Paul lives with his wife, Sherri, in Fair Oaks, California. They have two grown, married children and four grandchildren.

The Liquid Bible Is Also Available in Seminar Form!

If your church or organization is interested in hosting a Liquid Bible Seminar, or other training seminars available through *LEDR Coaching and Training*, just visit Paul's website at:

LEDR Coaching and Training
www.ledrcoachingandtraining.com

6172853R1

Made in the USA
Charleston, SC
23 September 2010